FINAL REPORT

ON

CURBING POLICE BRUTALITY: WHAT WORKS? A REANALYSIS OF

CITIZEN COMPLAINTS AT THE ORGANIZATIONAL LEVEL

This project was supported by Grant No. #98-IJ-CX-0064 awarded by the National Institute of Justice, Office of Justice Programs, U.S. Department of Justice. Points of view in this document are those of the author and do not necessarily represent the official position or policies of the U.S. Department of Justice.

November 30, 1999

ASTRACT

This project reanalyzes the data collected by Pate and Fridell (1993) on citizen complaints against police use of excessive force. The current report includes two empirical studies on the citizen complaints about police brutality in two mutually excluding areas: the police use of excessive physical force and the police use of all other non-physical forces, such as abuse of authority and verbal abuse. It attempts to establish the baseline correlation of citizen complaint rates with various police organizational factors, and to identify the causal effect of police brutality. Using Tobit regression technique, the research tested a series of hypotheses deduced from theories advanced by Wilson (1968) and Lundman (1980) with a number of control variables. It is found that organizational behavior and organizational characteristics are important covariates of the citizen complaints against police use of excessive physical force and police abuse of power. The police administration can influence its officer's behavior by strengthening the in-service training, paying attention to the education achievements of its officers, and actively provide best training for qualified new police in the force.

TABLE OF CONTENTS

CURBING POLICE BRUTALITY: WHAT WORKS? A REANALYSIS OF
CITIZEN COMPLAINTS AT THE ORGANIZATIONAL LEVEL

INTRODUCTION

Police officers have been granted the privilege of using "non-negotiable coercive force" (Bittner 1970) to control citizens' behavior and ensure public order. While the authority to use such force is not a problem, its proper application is "the central problem of contemporary police misconduct" (Kerstetter 1985). Empirical research on this central problem, however, is scarce. This is particularly true at the organizational level. Most previous studies on citizen complaints have been conducted at the individual level and focused on a limited number of jurisdictions, and the measures have not been consistent across studies (Dugan and Breda 1991; Kerstetter 1985; Littlejohn 1981; Pate and Hamilton 1991; Toch 1995; Wagner 1980; Wagner and Decker 1993; Worden 1995). The current report includes two empirical studies examining the two related issues of police brutality at the organizational level: citizen complaints about police use of physical force and citizen complaints about police use of nonphysical force[1].

Police use of excessive force is also called police brutality. Both terms refer to any unnecessary use of force by police. Reiss (1971:334) defines police brutality as any practice that degrades citizen status, "that restricts their freedom, and that annoys or harasses them," or that uses unnecessary and unwarranted physical force. Building on Reiss, Decker and Wagner (1982) modify the definition of police brutality as the citizens' *judgment* that they have not been treated with full rights and dignity by police as expected in a democratic society. The current study will use this definition to examine two categories of citizen complaints about police brutality: excessive physical force and abuse of police power[2].

While estimates vary, the incidences of police brutality are infrequent (Dugan and Breda 1991; Fyfe 1995; Kerstetter 1985; Klockars 1996; Littlejohn 1981; Pate and Hamilton 1991; Wagner 1980; Wagner and Decker 1993; Worden 1995). Even so, police use of excessive force is a serious problem, both for citizens who might be subjected to such force and for officers who employ it. Many riots of this century were caused by the public perceptions concerning the police misues of force, from the Chicago disturbance of 1919 to the Los Angeles riots followed the trial of police officers in the Rodney King incidence. Police use of excessive force reduces public confidence in the police, depresses officer morale, and generates conflict between police and residents (Langworthy and Travis 1994). The police agency's image can be tainted significantly by the conduct of its officers (Son et al. 1997). Johnson (1981) argues that perceptions of police brutality have been at the heart of citizen distrust of and complaints about the police. Investigations done by the Christopher Commission (1991) reveal that brutality is one manifestation of the often troubled relationship between the police and the communities they are supposed to serve and protect.

Furthermore, scandals associated with abuse of authority "jeopardize organizational stability and continuity of leadership" (Kelling, Wasserman, and Williams 1988), since the organization is at risk of outside interference, and the police chief is at risk of losing his or her job. Still another important point is that whenever police violate either the spirit or the letter of the law, the line between totalitarian and democratic governance becomes blurred.

Although the issue of controlling police use of excessive force is very important and theories about minimizing police misconduct are widely available, empirical research in this area is limited, particularly at the organizational level. At the individual level, Reiss (1971) has done a classic participation analysis of police use of force. Others have studied the extent and nature of citizen complaints (Dugan and Breda 1991; Kerstetter 1985; Littlejohn 1981; Pate and Hamilton 1991; Wagner 1980; Wagner and Decker 1993). More recently, Griswold (1994) did a multivariate analysis of the three factors on the disposition of complaints. Kerstetter et al. (1996) studied the impact of race on the investigation of excessive force allegations against police. Dunham and Alpert (1995) did a case study on controlling police use of excessive force in Miami. All these studies are informative and help to understand police brutality. However, few of studies report correlation of citizen complaints at the organizational level. While Griswold (1994) and West (1988) notice the paucity of empirical research regarding the factors that are related to the disposition of complaints and call for additional research, at the organizational level less research has been undertaken either about the nature of the problem or about the efficacy of proposed solutions.

The current study contributes to filling this gap primarily through reanalysis of data collected by Pate and Fridell (1993). Although designed to be a comprehensive national survey of law enforcement agencies on the matter of police use of excessive force, Pate and Fridell's final report (1993) does not fully use the information they have collected. The report covers three major topics: the extent of police use of physical force as recorded by police departments, the extent of citizen complaints about police use of physical force as recorded by police departments, and the legal consequences of using

3

excessive force. It presents a series of 2 by 2 contingent tables of statistics and bar

graphics. These tables and figures contain the raw numbers and sometimes percentages

of these interests. The independent variables are largely two: agency types and agency

size. It is doubtful, however, all these bi-relationships will endure the scrutiny of

multiple regression analysis. For example, city police have the highest citizen complaint

rate, and a lower percentage of officers with college degrees and a higher percentage of

black officers (Pp. 99-105). Whether the effect of police education on the citizen

complaint rate will be significant once the percentage of minority officers is controlled

for remains to be tested. Other information gained in their survey, including civilian

boards, effect of training programs, etc., is not utilized in their report.

In addition, this study develops a parsimonious multivariate statistical model to

test various theses on controlling police use of physical force and abuse of police power.

Multivariate analysis is superior to the bivariate analysis because it provides various means

to control for spuriousness, interpretation, and multiple causes. Not all statistical

relationships are true. By introducing an additional factor, the original statistical

relationship may disappear, eliminating the spurious relationship. Furthermore, in a

complex world, the causes of a particular social phenomenon is seldom unitary. The

multivariate model helps account for the part of variation that is due to other factors.

Finally, with the statistical controls, the multivariate model helps eliminate, or at least

reduce, the effect of confounding factors on a bivariate relationship. After an extensive

review of the literature on causes of police behavior, Sherman (1980) concludes that very

few of the bivariate relationships between police misconduct and its various correlations

have been elaborated into multivariate relationships with any of the other independent

4

variables. This study examines police department characteristics and the impact of various programs on the rate of citizen complaints, and thus fills the gap by extending bivariate analysis to the multiple variant analysis at the organizational level.

THEORY AND HYPOTHESES

The study of police brutality is important since it illustrates fundamental conflicts that arise from policing in a democratic society. Given the importance of the issue in improving police and community relations, many theories have been proposed for curbing the damaging behavior of police.

Wilson (1968), advocating police professionalism, identifies two models for controlling police misconduct: the professional model and the bureaucratic model. The professional model works by ensuring that only the best-trained, most honest candidates are employed as police officers. The bureaucratic model depends on the issuance and enforcement of rules and regulations through close supervision of police officer activities.

Lundman (1980) criticizes professionalism as a control on police misconduct. He suggests that professionalism, by focusing on the individual officer, ignore the social and organizational correlates of misconduct. Furthermore, professionalism is an obstacle to citizen control, since by definition a professional is one who has special knowledge and skills that the average person lacks. Instead, Lundman (1980) maintains that most police misconduct is a product of organizational deviance, so that what needs to be controlled is not individual behavior, but organizational climates. According to this thesis, police departments may have different rates of citizen complaints. The difference varies with the particular departmental characteristics.

The bureaucratic model has also been criticized for emphasizing negative rule enforcement. Goldstein (1977) argues for positive approaches to control police behavior: reward proper behavior and provide appropriate role models. He also stresses the importance of specific training aimed at preventing improper conduct and for avenues of citizen redress in order to reduce police brutality.

All these theories point out various ways that law enforcement officers' use of unnecessary force can be reduced by various departmental policies and practices. No empirical studies so far, however, have tested the validity of these theories. Thus, their utility is still assumed, not verified. Reiss (1971) has done a classic participation analysis of police use of force. Others have studied the extent and nature of citizen complaints (Decker and Wagner 1982; Dugan and Breda 1991; Kerstetter 1985; Littlejohn 1981; Pate and Hamilton 1991; Wagner 1980; Wagner and Decker 1993). Griswold (1994) did a multivariate analysis of the three factors on the disposition of complaints. Kerstetter et al. (1996) studied the impact of race on the investigation of excessive force allegations against police. Dunham and Alpert (1995) did a case study on controlling the police use of excessive force in Miami. Lersch and Mieczkowski (1996) investigated the characteristics of the officers and citizen complaints. All these studies are very informative and helpful to understand police brutality at the individual level.

At the organizational level, empirical research has not been undertaken either about the nature of the problem or about the efficacy of proposed solutions. Studies on citizen complaints have focused on a limited number of jurisdictions and the measures have not been consistent across studies (Dugan and Breda 1991; Pate and Hamilton 1991; Walker and Bumphus 1991; Wagner and Decker 1993). Many of these studies use a noncausal comparison approaches to test the citizen complaints and various characteristics of individual officers (Lersch and Mieczkowski 1996). Few of these studies report correlation of citizen complaints. Organizaitonal characteristics have not been used to predict citizen complaints against police use of excessive physical force. Sherman (1980) proposed that more research at the organizational level is needed since theoretically the macro level of explanation ought to be the most powerful level. Echoing Sherman, Wagner and Decker (1993; 1997) also argued that citizen complaints are most appropriate to be studied at macro-level rather than micro-level when considering efforts to stem police behavior perceived offensive by citizens.

The paucity of empirical research on excessive physical force at the organizational level is partially due to the lack of data in this regard. As Pate and Fridell (1993) noted, police use of excessive force is low-visibility act, many victims do not report such incidents, and many police departments do not collect information on such events. Further, from the police stand of view, complaints concerning the use of unnecessary force may be due to the fact that subjects have been arrested for a legitimate offence, or who have lurked by the potential of winning a big law suit. However, studies on the citizen complaints indicate that citizens did not file a complaint simply for a personal revenge motive (Russell 1978). There are obstacles to complaints, such as personal fear of reprisal, complex and cumbersome filing procedure, and the highlighted possibility of criminal prosecution for making a false report (The National Advisory Commission on Criminal Justice Standards and Goals 1973). Although not all citizens who are subject to unnecessary force will file a formal complaint which will end up in the police department and not all recorded complaints are legitimate, Bailey and Mendelsohn (1969) observed that willingness to file a complaint seems to be a function of what happens to people and what they expect to gain from it. Therefore, citizen complaints should be looked as a "barometer of police performance" (Wagner and Decker 1997) and as "important indicators of public perception of the agency" (The United States Commission on civil Rights 1981).

In this study, we use data collected by Pate and Fridell (1993), which were designed to be a comprehensive national survey of law enforcement agencies on the matter of police use of excessive force. Their data provide a national picture of police use of force as reflected by official records. Their own study, however, only provides comparison of simple percentages and bivariate analysis. Theories and hypotheses are not tested against each other in the multiple variate analysis. Further, Pate and Fridell (1993) attempt to cover a much wider variety of topics, from citizens' complaints about physical force, to internal complaints about physical force, to verbal abuse of power, and to litigations.

Our study, in contrast, focuses on citizen complaints against the police use of excessive physical forces and abuse of power. All aspects of police brutality defined by Reiss (1971) and modified by Decker and Wagner (1982) are included in the measures of police use of excessive physical force and abuse of power. Thus, the two measures include citizen complaints of police physical force, improper investigation, illegal search, intimidation, and verbal abuse.

Since both Wilson (1968) and Lundman (1980) suggested that organizational behavior and organizaitonal characteristics are potentially related to the citizen complaint rate against the police, we will test their theories. From Wilson's professionalism control thesis, we have reduced a number of testable propositions included in the following two sets of hypotheses.

Hypothesis 1: Psychological exams taking before admitting to police academy, field training officer programs, and the length of probationary period tend to reduce citizen complaint rate against police use of physical force and abuse of power.

As we know, police socialization begins at the police academy, and it continues in field training and throughout an officer's career. Hiring the best qualified officers as a control is advocated by Wilson (1968) in his professional model, and also by Alpert and Fridell (1992) in their recommendation for hiring suitable officers to defend against police use of excessive force. These arguments are more rhetorical than empirical (see Swanson 1977; Bowker 1980; and Sherman 1980). Our first set of hypotheses captures the concept of Wilson's professional model.

Hypothesis 2: Increasing the number of in-service training programs on the use of force within a police department, regular reviews of the use of force, written policy on the use of less lethal weapon, and the reporting requirement for the use of force are negatively related to the citizen complaint rate.

Our second set of hypotheses target the bureaucratic model in controlling police excessive physical force. Wilson (1968) and Goldstein (1977) advised police agencies to strengthen institute training specifically aimed at preventing improper conduct. More recently, Alpert and Fridell (1992) called for competent training to minimize the police use of excessive force. We shall test the effectiveness of these in-service training programs and regular reviews in reducing the police brutality.

Part of the problem in controlling police brutality is that what is and what is not brutality has not been clearly defined by the court (Alpert and Smith 1994) or by many police departments. Evidence regarding police use of the deadly force suggests that implementation of more restrictive policies decreases the use of deadly force (Meyer 1980; Sherman 1983). Since some police departments have written policy on the use of less lethal force and others don't, and some have mandatory reporting systems on the use of force while others don't, we shall expect those with written policy and those with mandatory reporting system to have fewer citizen complaints. The above four variables measure Wilson's bureaucratic model that the police misconduct could be controlled by the issuance and enforcement of rules through close supervision.

From Lundman's organizational product thesis, we also reduce two sets of testable propositions included in the following.

Hypothesis 3: The establishment of civilian review boards reduces the citizen complaint rate.

The control of police use of excessive force through civilian review board is widely hailed as a cure by a number of scholars (Goldstein 1977; Lundman 1980; Reiman 1985). West (1988:108), for example, stated that the closed system (or bureaucratic model of control), where police investigate the police, is contrary to "the rules of natural justice and is, by definition, imperfect." Some researchers doubt the effectiveness of civilian review board (Langworthy and Travis 1994). Its empirical efficiency has yet to be decided by empirical data.

Hypothesis 4: The composition of a police department's personnel is related to the citizen complaint rate. The larger the proportion of female and African-Americans in the department, the higher the educational level of police department personnel is, and the longer the average service years a police department is, the lower the citizen complaint rate becomes.

Individual-level data provided evidence that women officers may act to reduce the likelihood of violence in police-citizen encounters (Grennan 1987), they initiated fewer detentions and made fewer felony and misdemeanor arrests (Sherman 1975), and they are significantly less likely to have a citizen complaint (Lersch and Mieczkowski 1996). Individual-level data seemed to provide some conflicting evidence regarding minority officers. While minority group officers are found to be less antagonistic to the public and display greater ties to the community than their white colleagues (Berg, True, and Gertz 1984), they were more likely to use force, but less likely to use improper force in dealings with citizens (Worden 1995). Since gender and racial issues are at the core of our criminal justice system (Henderson et al. 1997; Cao, Frank, and Cullen 1996; Browning and Cao 1992; Browning et al. 1994), our study will test these associations at the organizational level.

Further, ever since August Vollmer, the police chief and reform advocate at the turn of the century, the education of police officers has become an increasingly important issue. In recent decades, there has been a concerted effort to raise the educational level of police recruits. The federal government has expended millions of dollars on law enforcement education (see Jeffery [1990] for a detailed discussion). It is argued that college-educated police officers are more sensitive to citizens, can communicate better, and are more effective (Hoover 1989). Past research indicates that average service years is expected to be negatively related to the citizen complaint rate (Sherman 1980;

Langworthy and Travis 1994; Lersch and Mieczkowski 1996). We shall test these hypotheses in our model.

Finally, our model controls for the environment of the police work in. It is expected that the population size and the arrest rate are both positively associated with the citizen complaint rate (Toch 1995).

METHODS

Sample

Pate and Fridell's survey in 1992 is by far the largest and most complete survey on citizens' complaints against the police misuse of force. Pate and Fridell used stratified sampling techniques to survey all state, county and local police agencies. Their data have been archived at NIJ Data Resources Program, the Institute of Social Research at the University of Michigan in the disk form (D000143) or CD form. They can also be downloaded directly into the personal computer from ICPSR's website (ICPSR 6274). The stratified random sampling results in the final sample size of 1,111 law enforcement agencies with complete answers, representing the overall response rate of 67.2 percent (for a detailed discussion of the sample procedure, see Pate and Fridell [1993]). The data provide a national picture of police use of force as reflected in official records and citizen complaints about the six categories of alleged police misuse of force. For our purpose, we only utilize the data of the municipal police departments. The response rate of their survey was 72.4 percent for city police departments (for a detailed discussion of the sample procedure, see Pate and Fridell [1993]).

The current study will utilize the part concerning citizen complaints against the police as recorded by each police department because the police own records of the use of force are extremely incomplete. For example, once information on the level of force reached "neck restraints," fewer than 70 percent of all police departments required a mandatory report. Such behaviors, as handcuffs and firm grip, have missing data as high as 90 percent (see Pate and Fridell 1993: 66-60). In contrast, information on citizen complaints about police brutality have only about 25 percent missing data (Pate and Fridell 1993: 89).

It is further limited to complaints about the city police departments because municipal police departments employ the majority of the American police, and it is at the city level that most citizens' complaints are generated (Pate and Fridell 1993) and that most citizens have contacts with their police (Langworthy and Travis 1994). Compared with centralized police system in continental Europe and Eastern Asia, American police is highly decentralized and is held for local accountability (Langworthy and Travis 1994; West 1988). It is, therefore, most appropriate to examine citizen complaints against the police at the municipal level.

Schafer's Norm is used to handle the missing data[3]. Although Schafer (1997) claims that the program is capable of dealing with missing data up to 50 percent, it is decided to be conservative on the issue and only included variables with missing data for fewer than 32 percent. After running the Norm, no missing data are assumed in the regression analyses.

Organizational approach has been very productive in sociological literature and this approach is adopted for analysis of citizen complaints against police use of force in this study. Many variables indicative of organizational characteristics and organizational behavior were created from Pate and Fridell's data to test Wilson's professionalism control thesis and Lundman's organizational product thesis.

Measures

Table 1 presents the sample characteristics in terms of means, standard deviations, range, and percentages of missing data of the ten variables. Also, percentage distribution of population served is reported.

--- TABLE 1 ABOUT HERE ---

Dependent Variables: There are two dependent variables in the current study. They are the rate of citizen complaints about police abuse of their power *per thousand officers* in a police department and the rate of citizen complaints against police use of excessive physical force *per hundred officers* in a police department. To provide standardized estimates for each police department, the citizen complaint rates are calculated, using the total number of citizen complaints in 1991 as the numerator and the total number of the sworn officers in a police department in that year as the denominator. The unfounded complaints are included in the analysis because to do otherwise would introduce yet another police discretionary decision[4].

The first dependent variable, police abuse of their power, is an index variable formed by five items taping the police abuse of power. The five items are 1) total number of citizen complaints about unlawful arrest/detention; 2) total number of citizen complaints about illegal search or seizure, 3) total number of citizen complaints about harassment and intimidation, 4) total number of citizen complaints about misuse of authority, and 5) total number of citizen complaints about improper language. To provide a standardized estimate for each police department, the five citizen complaint rates per thousand sworn officers is calculated for each of the complaint item, using the total number of citizen complaints in 1991 as the numerator and the total number of the sworn officers in a police department in that year as the denominator. The index variable consisted of the above five items yields a reliability of .69. The final number of city departments included in our analysis is 731.

The second dependent variable measures the citizen complaint rate about police use of excessive physical force per hundred officers. This only includes the complaint rate of police excessive, undue or unnecessary use of *physical* force. Pate and Fridell (1993) use the number of citizen complaints as one of the major dependent variables in their study while this study focuses on the rate of citizen complaints. For our purpose, we select a subsample of large city police departments with a cutting point at fifty employees or more (Crank and Wells, 1991). This further selection is warranted since large police departments are generally considered more bureaucratic and having better records than small- and medium-size police departments. The final number of city departments included in this analysis is 535.

To correct the skewed distribution of the citizen complaint rate against police use of excessive physical force, "1" is added to the dependent variable and it is then transformed into natural log form. The transformation reduces the effect of outliers and increases the likelihood of bivariate normality[5].

Independent Variables: There are fourteen independent variables derived from the hypotheses: pre-service psycho exam, Field Training Officer Program, length of academy, in-service training, regular review, less-than-lethal policy, report requirement, clinic requirement, close supervision, the civilian review board, education, gender, race, and length of service or average age of officers in a police department[6].

Pre-service psycho exam is a dummy variable with those police departments that require a psychological or psychiatric evaluation for all pre-service officers as 1 and those that do not require it as 0. The length of academy measures the number of months for completing academy training. Field Training Officer Program is a dummy variable on whether the department has a formalized Field Training Officer for the recruit with those having one as 1 and those not having one as 0. These three variables capture the concept that only the best qualified persons are recruited and they would receive prolonged and best available training before they become independent officers on their own.

The in-service training assesses whether a police department provides in-service training programs in the areas of use of the non-lethal force, use of deadly force, use of non-lethal weapons, and firearm requalification. This is an index variable and the Cronbach's alpha for this index is .84. The regular review is a dummy variable, asking whether the police department reviews and investigates use of force reports by officers even if no citizen complaint or civil suite was filed.

Less-than-lethal policy is a dummy variable with departments that have written policy for the use of less-than-lethal force as 1 and those that don't have such a written policy as 0. Reporting requirement is an index variable measuring whether it is mandatory for an officer to report the incidents of using force in a police department regarding the use of twist lock, bodily force, unholster weapon, swarm, firm grip, neck restraint, handcuff/leg restraint and come-alongs. The Cronbach's alpha for this index is .69.

Close supervision is captured with mandatory reporting to the supervisor about an incident as 1 and otherwise as 0. Seventy-six percent of the agencies require such reporting. Clinic requirement for filing a complaint is measured with those departments requiring as 1 and others as 0. Fifty-four of the departments have such requirement (see Table 1).

The civilian review board is a dummy variable with those police departments that have it as 1 and those that do not have it as 0. The composition of the police department—gender, race and education -- is measured by the percentage of female officers, the percentage of black officers, and the percentage of officers with at least a B.A. or B.S. degree in a law enforcement agency. Length of services or the average age assesses the average number of years served or the average age of all sworn officers in a police department at the time of the survey.

Finally, the two control variables are arrests and population size. The number of arrests refers to the average number of arrests an officer made with regard to the seven index crimes (excluding arson) plus weapon possession in 1991. The population size is an ordinal variable with the proximate population covered by a police department with 1= under 10,000 residents and 4=above 50,000 residents. More than half of police departments serve the population larger than 50,000 residents (see Table 1).

Research Design

The Tobit model was employed to do the analysis of the citizen complaint rate against police use of excessive physical force or abuse of power since about twenty-three percent of police departments have no citizens' complaints. Ordinary least squares model gives inconsistent estimates when the dependent variable has many zero values. Tobit is frequently employed to deal with such censored dependent variables because it uses two formulas to predict values of the dependent variable – one for cases at the limit value (zero in our case) and another for cases above the limit (Cao, Zhao and Van Dine 1997; Greene 1993; Tobin 1958).

RESULTS

There is substantial variation in the two dependent variables—citizen complaints about the abuse of power and against police use of excessive physical force. The mean rate about the abuse of power is 7.5, ranging from zero to 82 per 1000 sworn officers (see Table 1). The mean complaint rate against police use of excessive physical force is 6 per 100 sworn officers, ranging from zero to 82 percent (see Table 1).

To capture the variation of the citizen complaint rate about the abuse of power, the Tobit analysis is utilized. The results of the analysis are reported in Table 2. There are two equations in the table. In Equation 1, Wilson's professionalism control thesis was tested with eight variables plus two control variables. In Equation 2, variables derived from Lundman's organizational product thesis were added into the model, and the two theses were tested together.

In Equation 1, it is found that reporting requirement is positively related to citizen complaints about police abuse of power. This result contradicts the theory prediction, which hypothesized that the more strict the requirement, the fewer citizen complaints. Clinic requirement significantly reduces the citizen complaints. That is, those police departments that require a citizen to have clinic evidence before filing a complaint have fewer citizen complaints. The rest of the variables from Wilson's thesis are not statistically significant, although length of police academy and written policy are both in the predicted direction of the theory. One of the two control variables—population served--is statistically significant in relation to citizen complaints about police abuse of power, and the other control variable—the arrest rate—is not significant. The larger the population the police serve, the higher the citizen compliant rate is.

--- TABLE 2 ABOUT HERE ---

In Equation 2, five variables derived from Lundman's organizational product thesis were added into Wilson' professionalism control model. It is found that, controlling for departmental compositions, reporting requirement becomes insignificant while clinic requirement continues to be negatively related to the citizen complaint rate. The other variables from Wilson's thesis remain insignificant.

Among the five variables from Lundman's organizational product thesis, the average age of a police department is significantly related to citizens' complaints against the police. Police departments with an older average age tend to have a lower citizen complaint rate. Civilian review boards and other departmental components—such as percentage of females, percentage of African-Americans, and percentage with bachelor's degrees--are not significantly related to the citizen complaint rate. The control variable of population served remains significant. The larger the population the police serve, the higher the citizen compliant rate is.

The other dependent variable--the rate of citizen complaints against police use of excessive physical force—is also analyzed with the Tobit regression. The results of the analysis are reported in Table 3. There are two equations in the table. In Equation 1, the unique variables of Lundman's organizational product thesis is tested with two control variables. In Equation 2, the complete model of Lundman's organizational product thesis is tested.

--- TABLE 3 ABOUT HERE ---

In Equation 1, it is found, surprisingly, that the civilian review board has an effect on the rate of citizen complaints, but in the opposite direction as the theory would predict. That is, the establishment of civilian review boards tends to be associated with a higher rate of citizen complaints. A police department's educational level has no appreciable effect on the rate of complaints. Gender and length of service all are significantly related to the rate of complaints. The larger percentage of females in a police department tends to reduce the rate of complaints, and the longer the average length of service in a police department is, the lower the citizen complaint rate. Race is significant too, but its effect contradicts the theory's prediction. The larger percentage of African-American officers is associated with increased complaints. Both control variables, arrests and population served, are positively associated with the rate of citizen complaints. The more arrests a police officer has to make per year, the higher is the citizen complaint rate, and the larger the population served by the police, the higher the citizen compliant rate.

In Equation 2, the complete model of Lundman's organizational product thesis is tested with data. It is found that civilian review board and percentage of blacks continue to affect the rate of citizen complaints positively, and length of service is associated with the rate of citizen complaints negatively. The effect of gender on complaints is washed out. As predicted by the theory, formalized field training officer programs and in-service training programs are both negatively associated with the rate of citizen complaints. The police departments with formalized field training officer programs tend to have the lower rate of citizen complaints and in-service training programs reduce the rate of complaints. The rest of the independent variables, pre-service psycho exam, regular review, reporting to supervisors, less-than-lethal policy, and reporting requirement are not significantly related to the rate of citizen complaints. Both control variables remain significant. The more arrests a police officer has to make, the higher the citizen complaint rate is, and the larger population the police serve, the higher the citizen compliant rate is.

DISCUSSION

To understand better the citizen complaints against police and the organizational covariates of the citizen complaint rate, multiple regression analyses were used to study the phenomenon. Our results indicate that there is some evidence that both organizational characteristics and organizational behavior are important in predicting the citizen complaint rate. The citizen complaint rate is also influenced by the environment the police have to work in.

Our research is exploratory in nature and findings are tentative. This study represents the first quantitative effort in applying the organizational approach to the study of citizen complaints against the police. However, as mentioned before, our study relies on official data. As such, the results must be viewed as tentative. All the problems associated with official data apply to our study. There is further some uniqueness regarding to the official data on citizen complaints. For example, these complaints could be indicative of a number of departmental characteristics, including filing procedures and confidence of residents toward the police (West 1988). In addition, the concept of excessive physical force is totally defined from the citizens' viewpoint. With the vague phrase of the court in defining police excessive force (Alpert and Smith 1994), it is known that citizens tend to define it broadly while police tend to define it narrowly (Klockars 1996). Being reasonable to one side may be viewed as unreasonable to the other side as the acquittal of officers involved in King's incident demonstrates. Addressing the issue of data quality is beyond the scope of this study[7]. Thus, these complaints are better regarded as "a valuable source of management information" (Skolnick and Fyfe 1993, p. 231).

Furthermore, although the sample is representative and although we have many police departmental measures, the police jurisdiction's social and economic characteristics are not completely controlled for. Wilson (1968) and Sherman (1978) both argued that police behavior is part of the local political and social culture. Jacobs and O'Brien (1997) recently found that city characteristics are important predictors of policing killing. We do not know to what extent and how those characteristics might also affect citizen complaints. However, our data set is the best available on the topic of citizen complaints against police use of excessive physical force and it allows us to assess many explanations of the citizen complaint rate. According to Johnston (1984), estimates based on comprehensive models are less likely to be biased.

We use city police departments as the unit of analysis. This is a departure from the prior literature, which concentrated on the study of police behavior at the individual level. In contrast, by analyzing the organizational covariates at the municipal level and by employing more appropriate statistical model, our results, even though exploratory in nature, are robust and have contributed to our understanding of the citizen complaints and of police organizational strategies in reducing the complaint rate. Several points of theoretical importance are in order.

First, Lundman (1980) hypothesis that the civilian review board is a cure for police brutality is not supported by our data while Langworthy and Travis's (1994) suspicion that the civilian review board may not be that effective has found some evidence. The civilian review board as alternative external complaint review procedures, however, can not be disregarded easily in the future study of police use of excessive force. Its positive effect may be due to a couple of reasons. First, police administrations in general resist the civilian review board (Swanson, Territo, and Taylor 1993; West 1988), making it hard for the civilian review board to work properly and effectively. Only the worst police departments tolerate the establishment of a civilian review board, and our results may have captured the historical inertia of these police departments. Second, past literature further indicates that among existing civilian review boards, their functions, missions, formal structure, and operating policies vary considerably (Walker and Kreisel 1997). Third, the variable is highly skewed and not normally distributed: barely 9 percent of the police departments in our sample reported that they have a civilian review board. For these reasons, we think that a full evaluation of the effectiveness of civilian review board in reducing police brutality is yet to be determined and we should continue to support it as one of useful mechanisms to reduce police use of excessive force.

Second, the composition of police departments' personnel is an important factor in predicting citizen complaints. Even though the educational level of a police department is not significant and higher percentage of females seems to associate with the increased complaint rate of physical force, the average age of a police department is negatively related to the citizen complaint rate of abuse of power. Age and experiences are important factors in handling the delicate human relationship. We should also remember that police departments with better educated officers and with more female officers are in general more liberal and more reform-minded. These police departments also tend to be more open to citizen complaints and tend to keep better records. It is possible that those police departments with fewer BA and BS officers do not keep a good record of the citizen complaints and those police departments with fewer women officers are very hostile to citizens' complaints. Our results may have captured these effects.

Third, although none of the variables in the bureaucratic model are significant, we cannot argue that they are not important in understanding the police use of excessive physical force. Bureaucratic regulations are always the starting point for the significant change in organizations although these regulations are themselves not enough for any meaningful change in organizations. In other words, the regulations are necessary, but not sufficient, conditions for change in police behavior. There are many entrenched informal organizations of the police behavior that has long been observed (Bittner 1970; Crank 1998; Lundman 1979). Future studies need to pay more attention to the applications of the bureaucratic regulations within the police departments and the informal organization of the police.

Finally, our analyses seem to provide some support to both Wilson's and Lundman's theses. It is found that both organizational behavior and organizational characteristics are related to the citizen complaint rate. As many criminologists argue, many theories are complementary to each other instead of competing to each other or contradictory to each other (Bernard 1989; Cao and Maume 1993; Groves and Lynch 1990; Tittle 1989). Thus, versed differently and with different emphasis, Wilson's professionalism control thesis and Lundman's organizational product thesis should be regarded as complementary and effort should be made to integrate them. It is clear that Wilson's professionalism control thesis and Lundman's organizational product thesis, together with Goldstein's (1977) institutional training hypothesis, and Sherman's (1978) organizational reform theme share a core assumption: all recognize that the police administration is able to influence their officers' behavior. For example, police department should reinforce the FTO program so that the roockie officers will have a good beginning in their career.

In summary, this study has found that organizational behavior and organizational characteristics are important covariates of the citizen complaints against police use of excessive physical force and police abuse of power. The police administration can influence its officer's behavior by strengthening the in-service training, paying attention to the education achievements of its officers, and actively provide best training for qualified new police in the force. Future study is needed to observe the applications of police departmental rules in daily operation as well as whether our model can be extended to explain police brutality in operation.

NOTES

1. Since this report is a combination of two empirical articles, it is important to notice some variations of the measurement. For example, the dependent variable for the rate of police physical abuse of power is the percentage while the dependent variable for the rate of police abuse of power is per thousand officers.

2. In the original proposal, I suggested three categories of citizen complaints about police brutality: excessive physical force, abuse of police power, and verbal abuse. In doing the research, it is found that it will be more parsimonious to merge the latter two categories into one: abuse of police power.

3. Multiple imputation is a simulation-based approach to the statistical analysis of incomplete data (Schafer 1997). In multiple imputation, each missing datum is replaced by m>1 simulated values. The resulting m versions of the complete data can then be analyzed by standard complete-data methods, and the results combined to produce inferential statements (e.g. interval estimates or p-values) that incorporate missing-data uncertainty.

4. It is very difficult to substantiate complaints against officers due to the high evidentiary standards (Golstein 1986). Substantiation rate ranges between zero to 25 percent, with ten percent or less being the norm (Pate and Fridell 1993). It is argued that it is easier to win a civil suit than to have a complaint against a police officer found to be merited (Griswold 1994; Sparrow, More and Kennedy 1990).

5. In addition to the dependent variable, independent variables of arrest rate, percentage female officers and percentage African Americans and percentage officers with BA/BS degrees are in log form to correct for skewed distributions.

6.   Officers' average age and length of service are too collinear to be used in the same equation. The average age was used in analyzing complaints on abuse of power, and officers' length of service is used in complaints against police use of excessive physical force.

7.   The exact meaning of the term "compliant" is not constant across jurisdictions. Nor is the procedure the same across jurisdictions. Some police agencies require that complaints be formally recorded and processed regardless of how they are made (by phone, in person, through the third party, anonymously, by drunks, by persons under arrest), and run stings to assure that the rules are complied with (NYPD, Boston PD). Even in such places, however, there have been problems getting full compliance with even these most strict of procedures. Other police departments do not take complaints from many categories of persons (phone callers, third party, anonymously, by drunks, by persons under arrest). Some require complainants come into police facilities (often only during business hours), obtain complaint forms, take them home, complete them, have them notarized, and return a second time to hand deliver them to internal affairs or headquarters personnel. Some draw a distinction between "formal" complaints and "informal" complaints, do not record informal complaints (e.g. those made by citizens who call or come into police stations, having no idea that their complaints are being treated "informally") and do not require officials receiving "informal" complaints to inform citizens of the requirements for filing "formal" complaints that will actually be looked into and resolved (Lexington, KY comes most quickly to mind, but there are many others). Some require complaints to come into police stations and to state and file their complaints in the presence of the officers complained of (on an outrageous interpretation

of the theory that due process requires that officer be permitted to face their accusers). Others require complaints to sign their complaints under a typed notice that says (I'm paraphrasing the LAPD's long-time, but now amended, form that is still emulated by many police departments) "I have been advised that I may be sued for libel or prosecuted for filing a false official statement (a felony punishable by one year or more in prison.) if the statements I have made in this official report are not proven true by this department's investigation." Some allow receiving supervisors to decide that complaints are without merit, and to screen them out of the system without investigation. Some simply cannot give an accurate count of complaints because they have decentralized the system so that one receiving unit is not aware of complaints that have been received by others. In some places, distrust of the police has been so complete that people take their complaints to agencies other than the police, so that police agencies can boast that nobody complain about their officers. This was the case in Rizzo-era Philadelphia and, more recently, in New Orleans.

BIBILOGRAPHY

Alpert, Geoffrey P. and Lorie Fridell
  1992 *Police Vehicles and Firearms: Instruments of Deadly Force.* Prospect Heights,
      IL: Waveland Press.

Alpert, Geoffrey P. and William C. Smith
  1994 "How reasonable is the reasonable man?: Police and excessive force." *The
      Journal of Criminal Law & Criminology* 85:481-501.

Berg, B., E. Truce, and M. Gertz
  1980 "Police, riots, and alienation." *Journal of Police Science and Administration* 12:
      186-90

Bittner, Egon
  1970 *The Functions of the Police in Modern Society.* Chevy Chase, MD: National
      Institute of Mental Health.

Bohrnstedt, George W. and David Knoke
  1988 *Statistics for Social Data Analysis.* Itasca, IL: F.E. Peacock Publishers, Inc.

Bowker, L.
  1980 "A theory of educational needs of law enforcement officers." *Journal of
      Contemporary Criminal Justice* 1: 17-24.

Browning, Sandra Lee, Francis T. Cullen, Liqun Cao, Renee Kopache, and Thomas J.
Stevenson
  1994 "Race and getting hassled by the police." *Police Studies* 17(1):1-12.

Browning, Sandra Lee and Liqun Cao
  1992 "The impact of race on criminal justice ideology." *Justice Quarterly* 9(4):685-701.

Cao, Liqun, James Frank, and Francis T. Cullen
  1996 "Race, community context, and confidence in the police." *American Journal of
      Police* 15(1):3-22.

Christopher Commission
  1991 *Report of the Independent Commission on the Los Angeles Police Department.*

Crank, John P. and L. Edward Wells
  1991. "The Effects of Size and Urbanism on Structure among Illinois Police
      Departments." *Justice Quarterly* 8:169-85.

Cullen, Francis T., Liqun Cao, James Frank, Robert H. Langworthy, Sandra Lee
Browning, Renee Kopache, and Thomas J. Stevenson

1996   "'Stop or I'll shoot': Racial differences in supoort for police use of deadly force."
        American Behavioral Scientist 39: 449-460.

Decker Scott H. and Allen E. Wagner
1982   "Race and citizen complaints against the police: An analysis of their interaction."
        In *The Police and the Public*, edited by Jack Green. Beverly Hills, CA: Sage.

Dugan John R. and Daniel R. Breda
1991   "Complaints about police officers: A comparison among types and agencies."
        Journal of Criminal Justice 19: 165-171.

Dunham, Roger G. and Geoffrey P. Alpert
1995   "Controlling the use of force: An evaluation of street-level narcotics interdiction
        in Miami." *American Journal of Police* XIV: 83-100.

Fyfe, James
1995   "Training to reduce police-citizen violence." Pp. 151-175 in *And Justice for All:
        Understanding and Controlling Police Abuse of Force*, edited by W. Geller and
        H. Toch. Washington DC: Police Executive Research Forum.

Goldstein, Herman
1977   *Policing a Free Society*. Cambridge, MA: Ballinger.

Grennan, S.
1987   "Findings on the role of officer gender in violent encounters with citizens."
        Journal of Police Science and Administration 15: 78-85.

Griswold, David B.
1994   "Complaints against the police: Predicting dispositions." *Journal of Criminal
        Justice* 22:215-221.

Henderson, Martha L., Francis T. Cullen, Liqun Cao, Sandra Lee Browning, and Renee
Kopache.
1997   "Racial differences in perceptions of injustice." *Journal of Criminal Justice*.
        Forthcoming.

Hoover, L.
1989   "Education." Pp. 165-70 in *The Encyclopedia of Police Science*, edited by W.G.
        Bailey New York: Garland Publishing.

Jeffery, C Ray
1990   *Criminology: An Interdisciplinary Approach*. Englewood Cliffs, NJ: Prentice
        Hall.

Johnson, D.
1981   *American Law Enforcement: A History*. St. Louis, MO: Forum Press.

Kaminski, Robert J. and David W.M. Sorensen
 1995 "A multivariate analysis of individual, situational and environmental factors
    associated with police assault injuries." *American Journal of Police* XIV: 3-48.

Kelling, G., R. Wasserman, and H. Williams
 1988 *Police Accountability and Community Policing.* Washington, DC: U.S.
    Department of Justice.

Kerstetter, Wayne A.
 1985 "Who disciplines the police? Who should?" Pp. 149-182 in *Police Leadership in
    America: Crisis and Opportunity*, edited by William A. Geller. New York:
    Praeger.

Kerstetter, Wayne A., Kenneth A. Rasinski, and Cami L. Heiert
 1996 "The impact of race on the investigation of excessive force allegations against
    police." *Journal of Criminal Justice* 24: 1-15.

Klockars, Carl B.
 1996 "A Theory of Excessive Force and its Control." Pp. 1-22 in *Police Violence:
    Understanding and Controlling Police Abuse of Force*, W. A. Geller and H.
    Toch. New Haven: Yale University Press.

Langworthy, Robert H. and Lawrence F. Travis III
 1994 *Policing In America.* New York: Macmillan Publishing Company.

Littlejohn, Edward J.
 1981 "The civilian police commission: A deterrent of police misconduct." *Journal of
    Urban Law* 59(5): 5-62.

Lundman, Richard
 1980 *Police and Policing: An Introduction.* New York: Holt, Rinehart and Winston.

Meyer, Marshall W.
 1980 "Police shootings at minorities: The case of Los Angeles." *Annals of the
    American Academy of Political and Social Sciences* 452: 98-110.

Pate, Antony M. and Lorie E. Fridell
 1993 *Police Use of Force: Official Reports, Citizen Complaints, and Legal
    Consequences.* Washington, DC: Police Foundation.

Pate, Antony M. and Edwin E. Humilton
 1991 *The Big Six: Policing America's Largest Cities.* Washington, DC: The Police
    Foundation.

Reiss, Albert
1971   The Police and the Public. New Haven, CT: Yale University Press.

Schafer, Joe L.
1997   *Analysis of incomplete multivariate data.* New York: Chapman & Hall.

Sherman, Lawrence W.
1980   "Causes of police behavior: the current state of quantitative research." *Journal of Research in Crime and Delinquency* 17: 69-100.

1983   "Reducing police gun use: Critical events, administrative policy and organizational change." Pp. 98-125 in *The Management and Control of Police Organizations*, edited by Maurice Punch. Cambridge, MA: M.I.T. Press.

Skolnick, Jerome H. and James J. Fyfe.
1993   *Above the Law: Police and the Excessive Use of Force.* New York: Praeger.

Son, In Soo, Chiu-Wai Tsang, Dennis M. Rome, and Mark S. Davis
1997   "Citizens' observations of police use of excessive force and their evaluation of police performance." *Policing: An International Journal of Police Strategy and Management* 20: 149-159.

Swanson, C.
1977   "An uneasy look at college education and the police organizations." *Journal of Criminal Justice* 5: 311-20.

Toch, H.
1995   "The 'violence-prone' police officer," in Geller, W. and H. Toch (eds.), *And Justice for All: Understanding and Controlling Police Abuse of Force.* Washington, DC: Police Executive Research Forum.

United States Commission on Civil Rights
1982   *Who is Guarding the Guardians.* Washington, DC: USGPO.

Wagner, Allen E.
1980   "Citizen complaints against the police: The complainant." *Journal of Police Science and Administration* 8: 247-252.

Wagner, Allen E. and Scott H. Decker
1993   "Evaluating citizen complaints against the police." Pp. 275-291 in *Critical Issues in Policing: Contemporary Readings*, edited by Roger G. Dunham and Geoffrey P. Alpert. Prospect Heights, IL: Waveland Press.

Walker, Samuel and Vic W. Bumphus
 1992 "The effectiveness of civilian review: Observations on recent trends and new
      issue regarding the civilian review of police. *American Journal of Police* XI (4):
      1-26.

West, Paul
 1988 "Investigation of complaints against police: Summary report of a national
      survey." *American Journal of Police* 7:101-21.

Wilson, James Q.
 1968 *Varieties of Police Behavior.* Cambridge, MA: Harvard University Press.

Worden, R. E.
 1995 "The 'causes' of police brutality," in Geller, W. and H. Toch (eds.), *And Justice
      for All: Understanding and Controlling Police Abuse of Force.* Washington, DC:
      Police Executive Research Forum.

Table 1. Descriptive Statistics in the Analysis

Variables	Means	Standard Deviation	Range	% missing
The number of citizen complaints on excessive physical force per 100 sworn officers	5.96	6.52	0-82	25.23
The number of citizen complaints on abuse of power per 1,000 sworn officers[1]	7.53	5.98	0-27	26.81
Pre-Service Psycho Exam	.88	.33	0-1	13.13
Length of Academy	557.73	191.11	0-1050	19.02
FTO Program	.80	.40	0-1	12.86
In-service Training[2]	19.22	4.64	10-30	23.80
Reporting Requirement[3]	8.60	5.13	4-28	8.76
Regular reviews	2.54	.64	1-3	14.58
Less-than-lethal policy	.95	.22	0-1	13.08
Close Supervision	.76	.42	0-1	1.23
Clinic Requirement	.54	.50	0-1	1.09
Civilian Review Board	.09	.29	0-1	.50
Percentage with BA/BS	16.90	13.11	0-100	21.20
Percentage Females	5.50	5.30	0-38	1.78
Percentage Blacks	4.75	7.84	0-57	1.92
Average Age	36.16	4.04	14-51	23.53
Length of service	11.06	3.70	4-23	27.66
Arrest	7.58	7.93	0-60	28.45
Population Served	3.15	1.12	1-4	0.00

1=under 10,000 residents	14.0%
2= 10,000 to 24,999	14.6%
3= 25,000 to 49,999	19.5%
4=50,000 and over	57.9%

[1] The Cronbach alpha is .685 for this index.
[2] The Cronbach alpha is .842 for this index.
[3] The Cronbach alpha is .691 for this index.

Table 2. Tobit Analysis of Complaints on Abuse of Power
(N=731)

Explanatory Variables	Equation 1	Equation 2
Independent Variables		
Pre-Service Psycho Exam	1.33	1.41
Length of Academy	-.00	-.00
FTO Program	.83	-.25
In-service Training	.09	.09
Reporting Requirement	.10*	.08
Less-than-lethal Policy	-.47	-.96
Close Supervision	.33	-.23
Clinic Requirement	-1.54**	-1.32**
Civilian Review Board		1.53
Percentage with BA/BS		.04
Percentage Females		.46
Percentage Blacks		.48
Average Age		-.29**
Arrest	.49	.05
Population Served	1.08**	2.20**
Intercept:	-3.13*	-7.64**
log likelihood:	-2028.61	-2009.27

* $0.01 \leq p < .05$
** $p < .01$

TABLE 3. TOBIT ANALYSIS OF CITIZEN COMPLAINTS AGAINST POLICE
USE OF EXCESSIVE PHYSICAL FORCE
(N=535)

Explanatory Variables	Equation 1	Equation 2
Independent Variables		
Civilian review board	.35*	.39*
Percentage with BA/BS	-.00	-.00
Percentage blacks	.14*	.01*
Percentage females	-.01*	-.01
Length of service	-.04*	-.06*
Pre-service psycho exam		.18
FTO program		-.37*
In-service training		-.11*
Regular reviews		.00
Close supervision		-.13
Less-than-lethal policy		.24
Reporting requirement		.00
Arrests per officer	.22*	.21*
Population serviced	.38*	.41*
Intercept:	.25	-1.13*
log likelihood:	-688.19	

* p < .01